CW00723123

From God With Love

Adam Houge

Published by Living Tree Publishing, 2014.

# Introduction

Many years ago the Lord spoke deeply moving messages into my heart—messages to motivate me to a greater walk with Him. While sitting alone with Him, as it was, in the secret place, He would meet up with me and share His heart with gentle whispers.

Each of these messages were softly spoken but profoundly impactful. By them my life has been changed, and now I hope they will do the same for you.

I have documented these words for your edification. I am not speaking for God in this, although the words are written as if from His mouth and not mine. And neither am I claiming that each of these words are from God to you. Rather, I am saying that He shared them with me to change my heart. And now I hope to encourage you with the same by sharing His words with you.

Consider taking this time to be refreshed in His Spirit. Sit quietly in the secret place, and dedicate yourself to Him now. Do you believe He's worth your devotion? Let love compel you to draw nearer! And may He bless you with the same.

# Day One

# Renewing Your Vows

Beloved, be renewed to Me. Haven't I always been faithful? But there are times when you have erred in your ways. I do not look at these, for My blood covers them. Rather, My gaze pierces your heart to see whether you are having a steady reliance on Me or not.

Come sit in My presence, beloved, and be refreshed by My touch. I have long awaited your coming. I always desire the time you spend with Me alone. Being with you has always meant much to Me. Now let Me mean much to you, and pursue Me with a diligent heart.

Be circumspect to the scores of things that distract you. There are many ideas, thoughts, and troubles that bombard you throughout the day. Find your peace in Me, and do not let these captivate your thoughts. Let your mind settle itself upon My Spirit as you meditate on Me through prayer. But be diligent to do this throughout the day and not only in My secret place.

While I most certainly long for your attention in the stillness, My deepest desire is that you would carry the message in your heart and continue to walk in it as you meditate upon Me. I know that the activities of your life try to distract you when you leave My quiet place. You come and pour out your heart then step away to continue with your day.

Render your day to Me, and let Me be the center of it at every moment. Focus on Me through continuous prayer. Moses didn't climb down the mountain and get back to his life. For I was with him in a pillar of cloud and fire. I would come down to Him at My discretion and speak with him face to face. Even so, I desire to speak with you through My Spirit. I speak to you constantly, but you are not always listening. Many things captivate your attention and distract you from Me. I call you to let go of your distractions and focus on Me with a steady heart. Every idol begins as a distraction from Me. Nothing should take your attention away. If it does, then I will have no part in it.

If you do not keep your eyes focused on Me, then when the water rises, you will fall in. You will be distracted as Peter was. But do not let the noise of the wind carry your thoughts away from Me. Pray without ceasing today after your time alone with Me. Be earnest in your prayers, and continue to do this today.

I do not call you to only pray today but to continue in this heart forever. Pursue Me, beloved. For I pursue you with an undying love. Seek Me with the same! Keep a steadfast heart in prayer every day, and I will pour out blessings you could never begin to imagine.

If you do not ask of Me, how can you expect to receive? While I know your needs, sometimes I wait for you to approach Me to foster our relationship. By this you will learn that I am the essence of everything. I am the center of life and the source of it. You will learn to rely on My substance and to be satisfied in the abundance of My love.

## *Scripture for Thought*

"He who dwells in the secret place of the Most High Shall abide under the shadow of the Almighty." Psalm 91:1

"Seek the Lord while He may be found, Call upon Him while He is near." Isaiah 55:6

"I sleep, but my heart is awake; It is the voice of my beloved! He knocks, saying, "Open for me, my sister, my love, My dove, my perfect one; For my head is covered with dew, My locks with the drops of the night." Song of Solomon 5:2

# Day Two

# Have My Mind

Give Me your mind. Relinquish your thoughts and worries to Me. Do not let others think for you lest they lead you astray. Let Me lead you as My guidance is perfect. While I have given you a mind for wisdom and thought, do not be given over to having a mind of your own. If you are led by your own mind, you shall go astray through incomplete or wrong information. But I know everything, and nothing I say or do is with error.

Rest your plans in My hands. Render yourself to Me completely. Won't I lead you in a perfect way?

## Scripture for Thought

"As for God, His way is perfect; The word of the Lord is proven; He is a shield to all who trust in Him. For who is God, except the Lord? And who is a rock, except our God? It is God who arms me with strength, And makes my way perfect." Psalm 18:30–32

"'For My thoughts are not your thoughts, Nor are your ways My ways,' says the Lord. 'For as the heavens are higher than the earth, So are My ways higher than your ways, And My thoughts than your thoughts.'" Isaiah 55:8–9

# Day Three

# Let Me Light Your Path

Sit in My presence this morning. There is nothing I could want more than to guide you in My truth. I am the foundation of truth, and everything I write and speak is perfect. Find the foundation of My perfection laid out in the pages of My Holy Word. Read the Scriptures I so diligently wrote for you through My servants. I have preserved its pages and kept them immaculate through time. Even so, I call you this day to allow Me to create an immaculate heart within you through My Scriptures.

Seek Me in the word. I am waiting for you there in the pages. My Spirit will speak to you through them and make My words come alive. When He does speak, take note of these things for I am speaking things relevant to your life. Each of these things He shows you will be immediately practical for your walk. Take them to heart, and practice them today—not as mere, dry religion but out of love for our relationship.

Let My Spirit show you how to practice My Scriptures. He will show you how to apply them in your walk on a moment-by-moment basis. So be sensitive to His voice that He can lead you in the perfect way.

## *Scripture for Thought*

"But the Helper, the Holy Spirit, whom the Father will send in My name, He will teach you all things, and bring to your remembrance all things that I said to you." John 14:26

"However, when He, the Spirit of truth, has come, He will guide you into all truth; for He will not speak on His own authority, but whatever He hears He will speak; and He will tell you things to come." John 16:13

# Day Four

# Rest in Me, and Let Me Work

I have not appointed it to you to know your future or My exact plans. I do reveal them to you little by little as you walk with Me, so pay attention to My Spirit as we stride. But do not fret over what the future holds. Your future does not hold you, but I hold your future.

So rest in My grace, and I will carry you with a tranquil mind. Put your thoughts to rest, and do not allow your anxieties to corrupt your peace. Keep a steadfast gaze on Me, and I shall prepare the way for you. I will stir up the soil for you to plant. I will carve the mountains and lay out the straight roads—fully paved for you. The hard work is Mine, and all you need to do is learn to rest in My daily sufficient grace.

Wait for Me, and at the appointed time I will make your immediate future known to you. I will show you the road to take—the one I have labored hard to carve and pave. I will show you where to plant your seeds, having stirred up their hearts to receive them. Some shall fall upon poisoned ground, and the seeds will amount to nothing. But a few will land upon the loose, fertile soil of a heart well prepared by Me. It will produce one hundred fold in time to come. But do not pick and choose what field you sow your seeds in. I command you to sow them in every field as My Spirit leads you. If they reject your word, then at least they have been given the chance. Some who you would expect to reject My word will receive Me with tears and trembling. Consider My beloved Paul, who persecuted My people. Did He not fall in love with Me?

So still your mind, and let Me lead. Put your hand in Mine, and I will show you the way you should go.

## *Scripture for Thought*

"For now we see in a mirror, dimly, but then face to face. Now I know in part, but then I shall know just as I also am known." 1 Corinthians 13:12

"For as many as are led by the Spirit of God, these are sons of God." Romans 8:14

# Day Five

# I Suffer With You

I know your trials and your suffering, and your heart matters to Me. I did not promise that you would not have suffering in this life, but I have promised that I would carry you through it all because you are precious to me. I will bear your pain on My shoulders; when you hurt, I will hurt because I love you.

Yes, beloved, I will suffer with you. I can't stand to see the things you go through, but I know that they will benefit you in the end. I promise I will use them for good and tutor you through them. My lessons have eternal value, and all your suffering will be turned into rejoicing. I have allowed you to go through this because I knew that the mountain of your rejoicing would be greater than the valley of your pain.

I do not desire to see you hurt. If I did, then why would I seek to eradicate it at the end of all things? Beloved, I intend to wipe away your tears; only be faithful to draw near to Me and let Me comfort you now.

## Scripture for Thought

"In the multitude of my anxieties within me, Your comforts delight my soul." Psalm 94:19

"And God will wipe away every tear from their eyes; there shall be no more death, nor sorrow, nor crying. There shall be no more pain, for the former things have passed away." Revelation 21:4

# Day Six

# I Must Rule Over You

My beloved, listen to My Spirit, and let Me speak to you. I will lead you in unexpected ways and ask you to do things that would surprise you. But my love will never fall short. My truth shall never fail. I never will steer you wrong; I promise I shall never guide you amiss. Surrender to my guiding hand, and your ministry shall glorify Me for your ministry is My ministry. True ministry is to minister Christ to another. Am I not Christ? Let Me minister Myself to them through you. Beloved, be pliable in My hand. Let Me mold your future as the potter does the clay. Let Me decide what you shall do to serve Me.

Do not walk off while My Spirit is speaking. I deserve a servant who obeys My voice. Do not all masters tell their servants what they want them to do? Do not try to do what you think I want you to do, but do the things that My Holy Spirit tells you to do. Be obedient to Me for this is what I desire.

You must be completely flexible in this. You must be directed by My spirit as Paul was in his long journeys and as Peter was when I sent Him to the centurion. You must be as Philip was when he traveled along the desert roads through the direction of My Holy Spirit. My words shall bring light to My children. Therefore, beloved, let Me speak through you. I will teach you what you shall say and show you the things that you should do for Me. I am the Lord your God. I am your Master, and let there be none other beside Me. Yes, beloved, let not even your own heart rule over you. Do not choose what I would have you do. But humbly submit to My Holy Spirit as I lead you.

## Scripture for Thought

"For as many as are led by the Spirit of God, these are sons of God." Romans 8:14

"But if you are led by the Spirit, you are not under the law." Galatians 5:18

"Hear, my son, and receive my sayings, And the years of your life will be many. I have taught you in the way of wisdom; I have led you in right paths. When you walk, your steps will not be hindered, And when you run, you will not stumble." Proverbs 4:10–12

# Day Seven

# Trust in Me

There is nothing idle in the things I do. As a master artist, every stroke is essential to My creativity. As I prune your vineyard, you may be inclined to ask Me, "My Lord, what are you doing?!" But do not fear, My beloved. My every move is with purpose. A vineyard must be chopped with a machete. It doesn't seem artistic but rather ruthless. It is by removing the wasteful branches that you can be enabled to produce the most fruit. I shall likewise prune you in My wisdom.

Though not everything I do shall make sense to you, be subject to My guiding hand. My hand shall overshadow you and lead you in the way. Do not lean upon your own understanding, but trust in My faithfulness. I promise I shall never fail you. If I have told you to do something, then obey without question. If it was easy to see what I'm doing, then why would it be called blind faith? Blind faith is essential for the works that I call you to do. But know that I do this that you may learn to trust Me because trust is the cornerstone of every relationship. What has ever led you to believe that I am not trustworthy? Name My deed that was done wrongly! But if there is nothing, then why would you struggle with trusting Me?

Do not seek to do your own thing or question the stroke of my brush. Although it may not make sense to you, trust in Me. For I am God, not you. I see that which you do not see, I know what you cannot know, and I will lead you in these things that your way may be perfect before Me. Only let go of your plans, and do not question Me. Do not fear, for I shall guide you safely in the way. Although the darkness may surround you, I shall be a light to you. Sit in the presence of My light, and My guiding hand shall comfort you. Be sensitive to My Spirit. Discern His voice accurately. Be careful to listen for it because sometimes I whisper. Be diligent to listen, and you will hear all that I call you to do. Do not let the noises in your life interfere with My communication. Learn to have a sound mind even as I did while walking on the crashing waves. I will give you the soundness of mind, for it is Mine to give. I have the power and the authority to give you peace even in the worst storms of your life.

## Scripture for Thought

"Oh, taste and see that the Lord is good; Blessed is the man who trusts in Him!" Psalm 34:8

"For God has not given us a spirit of fear, but of power and of love and of a sound mind." 2 Timothy 1:7

# Day Eight

# Show Me Gratitude

Look at your life, and consider all that My hand has done for you. Show Me gratitude. Do I not deserve your praises? Praise Me out of the abundance of your heart. Love Me with the fullness of your soul. Rejoice in Me even as I rejoice over you. Worship Me today, and keep your mouth fixed on My praise. Speak well of Me to all men that they may know My sovereignty. Be diligent to honor Me in both your words and your conduct even as I have been diligent to love you.

Worship Me through your deeds. Do I not deserve them? Pour out your praise to Me in the fullness of your heart. Make it your solid effort to continue in worship. Speak to Me, and do not sing about Me. Keep our line of communication steady. True worship is communication. As you communicate the abundance of your heart and gratitude to Me, I overshadow you in the joy of My Holy Spirit. If then you want to be continually overshadowed by My Holy Spirit, continually praise Me. While My Spirit may always be with you, your heart is not always with Me as it ought to be. If it were, then you would not sin. But when your heart is with Me, then My joy in My power with you to overcome all things.

## *Scripture for Thought*

"I will praise You, O Lord, with my whole heart; I will tell of all Your marvelous works." Psalm 9:1

"I will bless the Lord at all times; His praise shall continually be in my mouth." Psalm 34:1

"And my tongue shall speak of Your righteousness And of Your praise all the day long." Psalm 35:28

# Day Nine

# If I Am With You, What Have You to Fear?

I call you to follow Me and obey My Spirit, but I have not left you to fend for yourself. At times it may feel as though I am not with you, but truly I am a shield to you. Trust in Me and, I will defend you. Who shall come up against your God and survive? Who shall challenge the Mighty One and walk away unharmed? Am I not a warrior who battles for your soul? Behold, My sword is drawn to defend you, and I will scatter your enemies before you. But My heart is wide open to love you. Is it not in My heart to save you? Is it not in My heart to conquer all your enemies, including death?

Behold, I entered for war into the place of the dead and have risen up victorious! I am God, and there is none beside Me! Which war have I ever lost? What enemy have I ever run from? My feet trample the wicked like grapes, fear and fainting are before Me, and coals are kindled by the wrath of My presence. If I, the Almighty God, am with you, then whom shall you fear? I will save you from every evil thing that comes your way. I will not relent until you have known and seen My love!

In the days of Moses nothing was allowed to touch My holy mountain. By My presence, I set the mountain on fire, and the earth trembled before Me. I am God, who shakes the heavens and the earth with My voice, and all who come against Me fall backward in fear. In My Day, the clouds will recede like a scroll, and the mountains will crumble at My feet. I shall descend to protect My people, and every mountain and island will be removed. Fire and billowing smoke are in the future of My foes. I am a terror to My enemy, but I am a joy to My friend. Therefore, My friend, remember that your enemies are My enemies and that I will defend you against them in My proper time. While no one could approach My mountain, I want you to approach My heart.

Come and seek Me, and see what I shall do! I will save you from every evil thing and bless you with peace in due time.

Yes, even your enemies, which take the form of trials, suffering, and hardship, I shall overcome by the might of My hand. I will overtake your trials with blessings that would make you forget the pain you've been through. I will wipe every tear from your eye and comfort you with My presence. I shall do all these things and more to bless you in My goodness because I love you. I am able to do all this, and nothing is too hard for Me. The only thing I require of you is that you believe.

## *Scripture for Thought*

"Beloved, do not think it strange concerning the fiery trial which is to try you, as though some strange thing happened to you; but rejoice to the extent that you partake of Christ's sufferings, that when His glory is revealed, you may also be glad with exceeding joy. If you are reproached for the name of Christ, blessed are you, for the Spirit of glory and of God rests upon you. On their part He is blasphemed, but on your part He is glorified." 1 Peter 4:12–14

"In this you greatly rejoice, though now for a little while, if need be, you have been grieved by various trials, that the genuineness of your faith, being much more precious than gold that perishes, though it is tested by fire, may be found to praise, honor, and glory at the revelation of Jesus Christ," 1 Peter 1:6–7

"My brethren, count it all joy when you fall into various trials, knowing that the testing of your faith produces patience. But let patience have its perfect work, that you may be perfect and complete, lacking nothing." James 1:2–4

# Day Ten

# Listen to My Voice, and Study My Word

Do you seek to please Me? Do you really want to make My heart rejoice? Then let Me tell you what I desire. I desire that you, My child, would walk in truth. For I have no greater joy than to know that My children walk in truth—not only in the truth of words and in refraining from lies but also in the truth of My doctrine, which saves your soul. Submit to My doctrine, and believe My holy word, not as you have been taught by men but as you have been taught by My Holy Spirit.

Rely on My teaching, and submit to it. My Spirit shall speak through men, and you shall be taught by them. But these words are not theirs; they are Mine. Therefore I command you to fear the words of their mouth and obey, even as I have commanded you to obey My word. Because My word is on their lips so long as they listen to My Holy Spirit and speak what I put in their mouth. Yet I call you to be discerning to know whether or not their words are from Me. And how shall you know this, My beloved? First by My Holy Spirit, whom you shall feel speaking through them, and second by My scripture.

Let My scripture be a foundation to you. Listen to My Spirit as you read your Bible, and I shall teach you from the pages. Learn to rely on Me as your elders rely on Me. Although they teach you the word, if you learn to rely on Me as they do, then I shall be your teacher even as I am their teacher; in time to come, there shall be no one above you accept Me. Then I shall set you up to preach peace to My children and speak the love of My covenant. But until then, humbly submit to My hand. Listen carefully for My voice, and obey it. For when I have spoken, whether by man or by burning bush or by My Holy Spirit, you are commanded to obey. So be diligent to listen to Me and equally diligent to study the Scriptures. Take some time to seek Me in the pages today.

Continue to do this every day even when you know My doctrine perfectly. Then you will be refreshed in My truth.

## *Scripture for Thought*

"I have no greater joy than to hear that my children walk in truth." 3 John 4

"But the Helper, the Holy Spirit, whom the Father will send in My name, He will teach you all things, and bring to your remembrance all things that I said to you." John 14:26

"These things we also speak, not in words which man's wisdom teaches but which the Holy Spirit teaches, comparing spiritual things with spiritual." 1 Corinthians 2:13

"But the anointing which you have received from Him abides in you, and you do not need that anyone teach you; but as the same anointing teaches you concerning all things, and is true, and is not a lie, and just as it has taught you, you will abide in Him." 1 John 2:27

"Take heed to yourself and to the doctrine. Continue in them, for in doing this you will save both yourself and those who hear you." 1 Timothy 4:16

"Till I come, give attention to reading, to exhortation, to doctrine." 1 Timothy 4:13

# Day Eleven

# You Have My Provision

Face each day with faith. For I, having planned ahead of you, shall provide. Set your heart to praise Me. My infinite resources shall provide for your sustenance, and they will never run out. Yes, My beloved, I shall take care of you; you have My promise—but only if you submit to My leading. If you run off to do your own thing and fall into a trial because of your sin, I will allow you to suffer this for your repentance. My special provision is not for the wicked but for the faithful in heart.

Yet I trust that you will not do this to Me. I know your heart is set on pleasing Me. If you desire to honor Me, then follow Me—not just the words I've written but the words I speak to you daily through My Spirit. Sensitize yourself to My voice, and I will lead you in the way. I shall provide for your needs in My timing. While your present may hold suffering and a trial, I have prepared your future with peace.

Whenever I save you from a trial, remember to worship Me for it. Take note of it, and exhort others. If any are weary and lacking faith, share how I've been faithful to you in your life and so encourage them. Show them My love through encouragement, and provide for them as I lead you.

Yes, I shall supply their needs through you and still give you more that you shall be taken care of. I always call you to take care of your brethren and to love them perfectly. But how I shall provide for them is up to Me, not you. So be sensitive to My leading, and I will show you a greater way that you may feed the hungry, clothe the naked, give homes to the homeless, and drink to the thirsty. Yes, you can do all these things through Me, and I shall sustain you. Only have faith in Me and stick to My plan.

## Scripture for Thought

"For we are His workmanship, created in Christ Jesus for good works, which God prepared beforehand that we should walk in them." Ephesians 2:10

"Therefore we make it our aim, whether present or absent, to be well pleasing to Him. For we must all appear before the judgment seat of Christ, that each one may receive the things done in the body, according to what he has done, whether good or bad." 2 Corinthians 5:9–10

"And let our people also learn to maintain good works, to meet urgent needs, that they may not be unfruitful." Titus 3:14

"This is a faithful saying, and these things I want you to affirm constantly, that those who have believed in God should be careful to maintain good works. These things are good and profitable to men." Titus 3:8

# Day Twelve

# Praise Me in the Storm

Why are you downcast, My child? Why is your soul disquieted within you? Hope in Me, and set your heart toward My praises. Do you want Me to rush in and comfort you, beloved? Then be diligent to praise Me. Have you not heard that I inhabit the praises of My people? Yes, praise Me in your hardship—even as Job did when he lost everything. He fell to his knees and worshiped Me, and I was a source of comfort to him.

Let My praises inhabit the dark places of your heart. I will enlighten you and lift up your weary soul. My Spirit shall overshadow you, and you will find the newness of My strength. Only be faithful to praise Me in pain, not only because I'm worthy but because you need Me. Praise Me out of faith. Worship Me because you believe I will make your circumstances better and that I am able to provide a beautiful future for you. By this, I will draw near to you because your heart draws near to Me.

## *Scripture for Thought*

"But You are holy, Enthroned in the praises of Israel." Psalm 22:3

"Though the fig tree may not blossom, Nor fruit be on the vines; Though the labor of the olive may fail, And the fields yield no food; Though the flock may be cut off from the fold, And there be no herd in the stalls— Yet I will rejoice in the Lord, I will joy in the God of my salvation." Habakkuk 3:17–18

# Day Thirteen

# Grow in Me

Be careful not to slip back. Although My hands hold you, do not slide back into the sins from which you came or allow idleness to creep up in your heart. If you love Me, then be diligent to grow in Me. Love is an action, not merely a word, so show Me that you love Me. A plant that does not grow cannot bear much fruit. I must bear fruit in you, and I have much to weigh on your branches. If your branches are thin and sickly, My fruit would likely break them. Thus I must have a strong tree on which to portray My fruit. Grow in Me, beloved, that you can bear all the things that I'm calling you to.

And how shall you grow? Through pursuing Me daily, praying to Me continually, worshiping Me in everything, listening to My Spirit and obeying always, and studying My Scriptures. Yes, study them hard as I teach you through the book. Glorify Me in these things, and the power of My glory shall be with you. Become the example of all that I am. And how shall you portray Me? With diligence of heart as you practice My perfect love toward Me and everyone else.

## *Scripture for Thought*

"Beware, <u>brethren</u>, lest there be in any of you an evil heart of unbelief in departing from the living God; but exhort one another daily, while it is called 'Today,' <u>lest any of you be hardened</u> through the deceitfulness of sin." Hebrews 3:12–13

"Now <u>the Spirit expressly says</u> that in latter times <u>some will depart from the faith</u>, giving heed to deceiving spirits and doctrines of demons," 1 Timothy 4:1

"And you, who once were alienated and enemies in your mind by wicked works, yet now He has reconciled in the body of His flesh through death, to present you holy, and blameless, and above reproach in His sight—if indeed you continue in the faith, grounded and steadfast, and are not moved away from the hope of the gospel which you heard, which was preached to every creature under heaven, of which I, Paul, became a minister." Colossians 1:21–23

"You therefore, beloved, since you know this beforehand, beware lest you also fall from your own steadfastness, being led away with the error of the wicked; but **grow** in the grace and knowledge of our Lord and Savior Jesus Christ. To Him be the glory both now and forever. Amen." 2 Peter 3:17–18

"Brethren, I do not count myself to have apprehended; but one thing I do, forgetting those things which are behind and reaching forward to those things which are ahead, I press toward the goal for the prize of the upward call of God in Christ Jesus." Philippians 3:13–14

"Now the ones that fell among thorns are those who, when they have heard, go out and are choked with cares, riches, and pleasures of life, and bring no fruit to maturity. But the ones that fell on the good ground are those who, having heard the word with a noble and good heart, keep it and bear fruit with patience." Luke 8:14–15

"Every branch in Me that does not bear fruit He takes away; and every branch that bears fruit He prunes, that it may bear more fruit." John 15:2

# Day Fourteen

# Prepare Your Heart to Praise Me

Rejoice always in Me! Not only in your victories but especially that I am faithful to lead you. As I lead you, you shall overcome all things, and victory will become natural for you. So do not praise Me in only one circumstance but glorify Me through continual obedience. You will find that I am with you always. Am I not the way in which you are called to walk? For I am the way; therefore follow Me. You are not My follower unless I am leading you. I must be in the front charging the way. But if you step ahead of Me, then you have taken a wrong turn! For assuredly I will not grant My strength to overcome for those who walk contrary to Me. Keep in stride while I pave the way. If you don't, I will be with you as I stand by your side waiting for your repentance. Then when you repent, I shall strengthen you again to follow Me.

So rejoice in My leading. When you hear My voice, know that I am guiding you. Set your heart toward My praise because victory and eternal life are right around the corner. Indeed, beloved, I am leading you to it, and I shall give it to you. Your heart is set on being faithful to Me, and all who follow Me shall inherit eternal life and abundant peace with Me. My child, I promise I will give you this; only continue to be faithful to Me, remembering that I will always be faithful to you.

## *Scripture for Thought*

"For as many as are led by the Spirit of God, these are sons of God." Romans 8:14

"But if you are led by the Spirit, you are not under the law." Galatians 5:18

"For we are the circumcision, who worship God in the Spirit, rejoice in Christ Jesus, and have no confidence in the flesh," Philippians 3:3

# Day Fifteen

# I Will Gather You to Myself

You are My jewel, and My treasure. You mean everything to Me. I promise you that I will take you to be where I am and that I will shower you with the abundance of My peace. I do not promise you that you will have peace in this life. On the contrary, I promise you that you shall have affliction because all who desire to live godly lives will suffer affliction. Yet I will be a source of comfort to you in your suffering that you can learn to rely on Me. And in due time, I shall return to save you from this world and give you peace even as I have promised you.

If a jewel was dropped in an open field, would not its owner return and search hard for it until he had found it? I tell you the truth, he would pitch his tent and set up camp, refusing to leave until he had gathered his valuables into his hand. Even so I shall be with you. I will part the heavens and search for you, and when I have found you, I will take you to be where I am with great rejoicing! The angels shall rejoice in that day that I have all My children by my side. When all is fulfilled, I shall give you a body that will never be corrupted or displease Me. Your work shall always be holy, and My heart shall always be pleased. But even now I see you as My finished work, like a jewel in My diadem. Yes, I will create you to be like a crowning glory to Me. For all the works of My hands shall glorify Me in that Day.

## Scripture for Thought

"Yes, and all who desire to live godly in Christ Jesus will suffer persecution." 2 Timothy 3:12

"Or what woman, having ten silver coins, if she loses one coin, does not light a lamp, sweep the house, and search carefully until she finds it?" Luke 15:8

# Day Sixteen

# I Shall Teach You

I will satisfy the deepest longings of your soul. For this reason, I sent My Spirit that you may experience My fullness. But unless you surrender to Him and His guiding hand, you cannot experience the depths of who I am.

Surrender to Me as I always call you to do. Pursue Me for I am already pursuing you. Open your heart wide to Me, beloved, and let Me take you by the hand. I have a path that I paved for you that is too difficult for you to understand. Yet I will teach you every step of the way that once you've walked along the road with Me, you'll be able to look back with wisdom.

Although you look forward without understanding, you shall look backward with perfect knowledge. I shall teach you because I love you, and My teaching shall lead you to eternal life. Therefore surrender to My words and take them to heart. Walk them out as I supply them. Be sensitive to Me and to My lessons. Daily I am teaching you something. If you are not constantly learning new things, then you are not listening to Me.

Examine your heart, and you tell Me with an honest face. Are you committed to learning and growing as you ought to be? Listen to My conviction, and pursue Me with your whole heart as I have already given My whole heart to you. Be faithful to love Me, stay sensitive to My daily lesson, and as you learn, you'll begin to understand the roads I've called you to walk on. Listen to My lesson, and I shall teach you until you have completed the subject. After you have learned the subject, I will create a new season in your life and continue a new subject, lesson by lesson, day by day. Be faithful to submit to Me in this and grow constantly.

## *Scripture for Thought*

"It is written in the prophets, 'And they shall all be taught by God.' Therefore everyone who has heard and learned from the Father comes to Me." John 6:45

# Day Seventeen

# The Cost of Complacency

I have called you to count the cost. Now I command you to consider it. Should you build then cease from building? Should you construct only to give up by a lazy hand? Watch yourself, and be circumspect to your actions. Continue to grow in Me as I have commanded you. Pursue Me and My Scripture, and be diligent to find Me there. The authority of My word cannot be replaced. Therefore do not allow the idle things of this life to replace My relationship with you. Am I not worth more to you? Then show Me by diligently loving Me.

I despise a complacent heart. It is unable to be motivated to action. I must have a heart that can be moved by My love to obey. Love in itself is an action. Therefore be fervent for Me, and be diligent to walk in My compassion toward others. Have you seen a suffering brother? Then refresh them. Become the image of who I am. Wouldn't I refresh them? What would I do for them? Would I not deliver them until I have completely satisfied all their needs? Do the same as I do, and let your heart be moved to compassion as I am always moved for you. Be My tool, and let Me use you to express My love to others.

Do not let complacency have its place in the corners of your heart. Keep it far from you, and always seek to grow in our relationship and in practicing My love towards others.

## *Scripture for Thought*

"Nevertheless I have this against you, that you have left your first love. Remember therefore from where you have fallen; repent and do the first works, or else I will come to you quickly and remove your lampstand from its place—unless you repent." Revelation 2:4–5

"I know your works, that you are neither cold nor hot. I could wish you were cold or hot. So then, because you are lukewarm, and neither cold nor hot, I will vomit you out of My mouth. Because you say, 'I am rich, have become wealthy, and have need of nothing'—and do not know that you are wretched, miserable, poor, blind, and naked—I counsel you to buy from Me gold refined in the fire, that you may be rich; and white garments, that you may be clothed, that the shame of your nakedness may not be revealed; and anoint your eyes with eye salve, that you may see. As many as I love, I rebuke and chasten. Therefore be zealous and repent." Revelation 3:15–19

"For the turning away of the simple will slay them, And the complacency of fools will destroy them; But whoever listens to me will dwell safely, And will be secure, without fear of evil." Proverbs 1:32–33

"Therefore, as we have opportunity, let us do good to all, especially to those who are of the household of faith." Galatians 6:10

# Day Eighteen

# Be Content With My Supply

Be content with My providence. Do not allow your anxieties to carry your heart. For you would wish to have more than I give you, and your soul would desire it. Fear sets in when I do not provide enough for you to keep the things you want. But find your contentment with the things that come down from above. My daily providence is sufficient for you.

Live according to My supply. Truly it is endless, but your flesh would lust for more. I do not call you to be complacent in poverty as you should expect My hand to deliver you. Wait for that day, and rejoice when it comes. But until then, be content with what I give you lest, through desire, you should sin. Do not desire the things that I do not have for you.

If you should want more than I give you, then you would be living for this world. Like a seed thrown among thorns, so you, My beloved, would become choked by the cares of this life. Do not let this happen to you; settle your heart in peace. Wait for My saving strength, and I will give you according to your need and supply your heart with joy. I will indeed give you some of the things you want but not everything. Your heart is not always right nor does it always align with Mine. But where our hearts meet, you will find My blessing waiting for you.

## *Scripture for Thought*

"Let your conduct be without covetousness; be content with such things as you have. For He Himself has said, 'I will never leave you nor forsake you.' So we may boldly say: 'The Lord is my helper; I will not fear. What can man do to me?'" Hebrews 13:5–6

"Trust in the Lord, and do good; Dwell in the land, and feed on His faithfulness. Delight yourself also in the Lord, And He shall give you the desires of your heart." Psalm 37:3–4

"And if we know that He hears us, whatever we ask, we know that we have the petitions that we have asked of Him." 1 John 5:15

# Day Nineteen

# Be Clothed With Humility

Who is there besides Me? Who has measured the waters in the hollow of His hand and weighed the dust of the earth in scales? Who sends forth the lightning and commands the whirlwind and tempest? Who raises and lowers the sea and floods the land? Who rules from Heaven's throne with a voice like thunder that shakes the foundations of the earth? Do not I, the Lord?

But in all My power and glory, I counted it as nothing for your sake. I humbled Myself through love that by My convicting kindness, I could receive you as My own. If then I, the Lord of glory, would so humble himself to serve you, how much more should you My servant humble yourself to serve and glorify Me? Commit yourself to humility, and submit to My guiding hand. Lay down your life, and take up My reward for you. Remember your fellow servants, for they are your family. Feed them with kindness, and clothe them with love. If I so loved you, then you ought also to love your brethren.

I, the Lord, shrouded Myself in humility and covered Myself with your shame. How much more should you, My beloved, be clothed with humility that I can cover you with My glory? Submit to a humble heart, and be content with such things as you have. Open your heart wide to Me that we can be renewed daily in our relationship. Seek Me, and meditate on My presence today.

## *Scripture for Thought*

"Let this mind be in you which was also in Christ Jesus, who, being in the form of God, did not consider it robbery to be equal with God, but made Himself of no reputation, taking the form of a bondservant, and coming in the likeness of men. And being found in appearance as a man, He humbled Himself and became obedient to the point of death, even the death of the cross. Therefore God also has highly exalted Him and given Him the name which is above every name, that at the name of Jesus every knee should bow, of those in heaven, and of those on earth, and of those under the earth, and that every tongue should confess that Jesus Christ is Lord, to the glory of God the Father." Philippians 2:5–11

# Day Twenty

# All My Roads End in Blessing and Honor

The lion is majestic when it walks, and it knows no fear. The cheetah is proud of its speed, and the deer strides with grace. The flowers of the field are clothed with beauty and are naturally fragrant. If I have given these their glory, how much more will I clothe you in honor? Yes, My child, your body of flesh has been sown in dishonor, but you will be harvested in honor. The beauty of your works and the fragrance of your deeds shall be perfect before Me. You shall know no fear and walk in majesty. No one and nothing shall make you afraid, and hunger will never overtake you. You shall know peace for all your days, and gladness of heart will be yours to the full. But before honor, there is humility.

Surrender to Me, My child. Aren't My plans greater? Although life may be difficult, I will create a new future for you before My face. You shall walk in my presence and I in yours. You will see Me, know Me face to face, and rest in My arms. Remember My plan for you, and surrender to it today. Humble yourself under My mighty hand, and in due time, I shall exalt you. While there may be pains in this life, My way is still greater. For it leads to everlasting life and peace with an abundance of joy.

What can you begin to image that I have not already known? Why would you seek to devise plans that are not of My will or of My doing? Behold, I have seen your face. Before your mother was born, I knew your name. I knew your deeds and heard your thoughts. Before you were born, I heard your first cry. For My hand has made you, and I have known everything there is to know about you before I created time.

I have known the things you would plan, and I tell you the truth: My way is still greater. Trust in Me, and lean not on your own understand. In all your ways acknowledge Me, laying your thoughts and goals before Me. Some of them I have laid on your heart, while others are not of My devising. Be careful to submit to Me. Seek My will, and I shall make you know it. Then when you have found it, I command you to walk in it.

All My roads end in blessing and honor. But the roads of the human heart always lead to disaster. Submit to Me, and I shall clothe you in beauty, and your fragrance shall be naturally pleasing to Me.

## Scripture for Thought

"'For My thoughts are not your thoughts, Nor are your ways My ways,' says the Lord. 'For as the heavens are higher than the earth, So are My ways higher than your ways, And My thoughts than your thoughts.'" Isaiah 55:8–9

"Trust in the Lord with all your heart, And lean not on your own understanding; In all your ways acknowledge Him, And He shall direct your paths." Proverbs 3:5–6

"I traverse the way of righteousness, In the midst of the paths of justice," Proverbs 8:20

"The Lord brings the counsel of the nations to nothing; He makes the plans of the peoples of no effect. The counsel of the Lord stands forever, The plans of His heart to all generations." Psalm 33:10–11

"There are many plans in a man's heart, Nevertheless the Lord's counsel—that will stand." Proverbs 19:21

"Uphold my steps in Your paths, That my footsteps may not slip." Psalm 17:5

"You will show me the path of life; In Your presence is fullness of joy; At Your right hand are pleasures forevermore." Psalm 16:11

# Day Twenty-One

# Do Not Look Back

Always test yourself. Watch your steps carefully to be certain you aren't walking off course. Keep your eyes fixed on Me and My goals for you. I will help you accomplish all that I require of you. I will be your strength, and My Spirit shall go before you. Did I not go before Israel as I led them into the Promised Land? When did they suffer defeat? When they looked back to Egypt, complained against Me, or had sin in the camp.

These things were literal but documented for your edification. Israel became a real and living parable for your life. Do not look back to the things of this world but keep steady on our journey. Did I feed them with delectable delicacies? No, but with manna, and My provision was sufficient. I am the bread that has come out of heaven; live by My word, and obey My voice. You shall not live by bread alone but by every word that proceeds out of My mouth. Listen, therefore, that you may hear My whispers. Read My doctrine, and study it diligently. For there is no greater authority of truth than My word—both what is written and what I speak to you daily.

Read My word today, and be sensitive to the voice of My Holy Spirit.

## *Scripture for Thought*

"Now it shall come to pass, if you diligently obey the voice of the Lord your God, to observe carefully all His commandments which I command you today, that the Lord your God will set you high above all nations of the earth." Deuteronomy 28:1

"Now therefore, if you will indeed obey My voice and keep My covenant, then you shall be a special treasure to Me above all people; for all the earth is Mine." Exodus 19:5

"This Book of the Law shall not depart from your mouth, but you shall meditate in it day and night, that you may observe to do according to all that is written in it. For then you will make your way prosperous, and then you will have good success." Joshua 1:8

# Day Twenty-Two

# Keep My Pace

Keep pace with Me, My child. Do not lag behind, but stay at My side. Follow Me, not from a distance but close by My side. I will protect you with you near to Me and show you the right course to take. My ways are wisdom, and My walk is perfect. Let Me teach you, and be pliable in My hands.

## Scripture for Thought

"As for God, His way is perfect; The word of the Lord is proven; He is a shield to all who trust in Him." Psalm 18:30

# Day Twenty-Three

# Be Perfect in Your Doctrine

Pursue my truth, and live diligently in it. I do not reveal My secrets to anyone but My children. Keep the tradition of My honor by walking in and preaching My truth. Many say amen and claim to walk in truth, but do not test their feet. Look at your feet, My child, and consider your walk. You are but flesh, and it is natural for you to stray. If you are not diligent to seek out and live in My truth, it will not come to you naturally. You must be intentional about finding it. I am not found in the doctrines of the organized church. I do not agree with the discord among the separate bodies. For they all claim to have My truth but believe different things.

Their core values are not sufficient for Me. None of My ways transgress, and I expect purity from My children. Be perfect in your doctrine. It won't be hard for you, because I will explain the perfect truth of my Bible through My Holy Spirit. All you need to do is listen to Me. So don't listen to your own heart but listen to Mine instead. Test yourself continually to see whether you are submitting to My Spirit and pursuing Me as you ought. I will lead you into all truth if you submit to My voice.

## *Scripture for Thought*

"Lead me in Your truth and teach me, For You are the God of my salvation; On You I wait all the day." Psalm 25:5

"However, when He, the Spirit of truth, has come, He will guide you into all truth; for He will not speak on His own authority, but whatever He hears He will speak; and He will tell you things to come." John 16:13

"Take heed to yourself and to the doctrine. Continue in them, for in doing this you will save both yourself and those who hear you." 1 Timothy 4:16

# Day Twenty-Four

# Humility Increases Strength

Come to Me with a teachable spirit. I cannot make use of those who disregard My ways and My truths. How can you grow unless you earnestly seek My teaching? How can you increase in My strength unless you diligently grow in your faith? Beloved, take My words to heart, and follow in My ways.

I cannot teach you unless you confess your limitations. Examine your heart constantly for this. If you do not walk in humility, you will never understand how fragile you are. But by humility, I will increase your strength. In your weaknesses, I will give you power. But first give the glory to whom it is due. Is not the glory rightfully Mine? Render it to Me in truth, and humble your spirit. I will make you to overcome trials, overpower your sin, and even trample death. For I am able to do these things, if you submit to Me. Let Me show you My ways. Open your heart wide to Me, and seek My teaching. If you pray for it continually with an earnest heart, My Holy Spirit will supply you with My abundant wisdom in truth.

## *Scripture for Thought*

"The fear of the Lord is the instruction of wisdom, And before honor is humility." Proverbs 15:33

"He who speaks from himself seeks his own glory; but He who seeks the glory of the One who sent Him is true, and no unrighteousness is in Him." John 7:18

# Day Twenty-Five

# Be Content With My Supply

Behold, I will come riding on the clouds of heaven with great glory and power. In My Day, I shall dissolve the elements, and the world that now is shall be known no longer. In the days of the flood, I washed the earth of its sin, but now I will purify it with My holy fire. All things shall be destroyed to make way for a new heavens and a new earth. But you, My beloved, I will carry safely in My arms.

Knowing that this world shall be dissolved by fire, what manner of person should you be when conducting yourself in godly fear and holiness? Do not cling to the things of this life; they shall be gone. There is nothing here that now is that won't be changed. Do not live for this present life, but live for Me! I am your only shelter in My judgment. You shall not find safety anywhere else. Do not say in your heart, "I am safe for you are My Savior," if you yet cling to the cares and idols of this life. You, My beloved, may suffer loss. Do not toss out your heavenly treasures. You can't imagine their immense value. Toss out the unnecessary excess in this life that your flesh has lusted for. Be sober in your Spirit, and take only the things I give you.

If I give you abundance, do not trust in it. Rejoice in My present joy knowing that what you now have will be destroyed to make way for a greater blessing. Every current blessing must be removed that a new and greater blessing may be added to you. Knowing this, expect to have trials and loss in this life while I prepare something better for you.

My child, do not be sorrowful if your current blessings are removed and you suffer loss. But retain in your heart and in your mind that I am preparing you for a greater blessing that involves My peace.

## *Scripture for Thought*

"Therefore, since all these things will be dissolved, what manner of persons ought you to be in holy conduct and godliness, looking for and hastening the coming of the day of God, because of which the heavens will be dissolved, being on fire, and the elements will melt with fervent heat? Nevertheless we, according to His promise, look for new heavens and a new earth in which righteousness dwells." 2 Peter 3:11–13

"Let your conduct be without covetousness; be content with such things as you have. For He Himself has said, "I will never leave you nor forsake you." Hebrews 13:5

"Now godliness with contentment is great gain. For we brought nothing into this world, and it is certain we can carry nothing out. And having food and clothing, with these we shall be content. But those who desire to be rich fall into temptation and a snare, and into many foolish and harmful lusts which drown men in destruction and perdition. For the love of money is a root of all kinds of evil, for which some have strayed from the faith in their greediness, and pierced themselves through with many sorrows." 1 Timothy 6:6–10

# Day Twenty-Six

# My Love Corrects

O My child, do not despise the chastening of your Father. I chastise the child I love. Because I care intimately about your life, I discipline you to keep you on course with Me. My rod leads you to salvation. Do not hate it. Embrace it. Accept My rod freely on your back. I will never give you more than you need nor more than you can bear. But I also never give you less than you need so that you may repent.

I am the perfect Father, who gives My children exactly what they need. When you step off My path, expect My rod and My staff to steer you back. If then you do not want My rod, follow Me faithfully as you ought. Listen to My voice, and do not brush it off. It is easy to do with the noise around you. But I call you to find an internal peace in your heart and meditate on My words. Walk by them, and they shall be a light to you.

## *Scripture for Thought*

"Yea, though I walk through the valley of the shadow of death, I will fear no evil; For You are with me; Your rod and Your staff, they comfort me." Psalm 23:4

"My son, do not despise the chastening of the Lord, Nor detest His correction; For whom the Lord loves He corrects, Just as a father the son in whom he delights." Proverbs 3:11–12

# Day Twenty-Seven

# Do Not Be Shaken

I anticipate your dependence on Me. I know your needs and when they shall arise. Your storms never shake Me, because I command them. Abandon your boat, and walk on the waves with Me. The vessel shall soon be overtaken by the waves, but in My hands, you shall be safe. Walk, therefore, by faith. I can do all things, and through faith in My voice, you can do all things.

Do not be shaken by need. Pray to Me, for I am already aware of your situation. At the voice of your prayer, I shall set your providence in motion. I have been preparing since before your circumstances befell you. I knew in advance, and My hand was working diligently to save you before you ever knew that tragedy would strike. My love shall lead you, and by My hand I will provide. Only follow My Spirit's voice and stay close by My side. Though trials may ensue, these are merely to test you. If you obey My voice, calamity will never destroy you. You shall walk away a stronger person than when you entered. Therefore rejoice in your trials because, by them, I make you strong in your faith, and through them, I will develop a more intimate relationship with you.

## *Scripture for Thought*

"And when the disciples saw Him walking on the sea, they were troubled, saying, 'It is a ghost!' And they cried out for fear. But immediately Jesus spoke to them, saying, 'Be of good cheer! It is I; do not be afraid.' And Peter answered Him and said, 'Lord, if it is You, command me to come to You on the water.' So He said, 'Come.' And when Peter had come down out of the boat, he walked on the water to go to Jesus. But when he saw that the wind was boisterous, he was afraid; and beginning to sink he cried out, saying, 'Lord, save me!' And immediately Jesus stretched out His hand and caught him, and said to him, 'O you of little faith, why did you doubt?'" Matthew 14:26–31

"Trust in the Lord, and do good; Dwell in the land, and feed on His faithfulness." Psalm 37:3

"Therefore I say to you, do not worry about your life, what you will eat or what you will drink; nor about your body, what you will put on. Is not life more than food and the body more than clothing? Look at the birds of the air, for they neither sow nor reap nor gather into barns; yet your heavenly Father feeds them. Are you not of more value than they? Which of you by worrying can add one cubit to his stature? So why do you worry about clothing? Consider the lilies of the field, how they grow: they neither toil nor spin; and yet I say to you that even Solomon in all his glory was not arrayed like one of these. Now if God so clothes the grass of the field, which today is, and tomorrow is thrown into the oven, will He not much more clothe you, O you of little faith? Therefore do not worry, saying, 'What shall we eat?' or 'What shall we drink?' or 'What shall we wear?' For after all these things the Gentiles seek. For your heavenly Father knows that you need all these things. But seek first the kingdom of God and His righteousness, and all these things shall be added to you." Matthew 6:25–33

# Day Twenty-Eight

# Labor in the Seeds

Do not strive for fruit, but labor in the seeds. There are many that seek to please Me by walking in legalism and practicing My Holy Scripture without My Spirit's direction. Submit to My Spirit, and focus on sowing the seeds. Sow in Me and My Spirit, and you will reap an eternal harvest.

Let My Spirit guide you, and focus on His word. He shall lead you in the way safely and deliver you from every harmful thing. Though trials may come, He will save you. Do not fear; you shall not be destroyed. But I will preserve you with My righteous right hand.

If you want to produce much fruit for Me, then do not focus on growing the fruit itself. Planting a single seed creates a greater harvest than focusing on growing one large fruit.

## *Scripture for Thought*

"The righteous shall flourish like a palm tree, He shall grow like a cedar in Lebanon. Those who are planted in the house of the Lord Shall flourish in the courts of our God. They shall still bear fruit in old age; They shall be fresh and flourishing," Psalm 92:12–14

"Do not be deceived, God is not mocked; for whatever a man sows, that he will also reap. For he who sows to his flesh will of the flesh reap corruption, but he who sows to the Spirit will of the Spirit reap everlasting life. And let us not grow weary while doing good, for in due season we shall reap if we do not lose heart." Galatians 6:7–9

# Day Twenty-Nine

# I Shall Carry You in Peace

Rest in Me. Let not any anxieties arise in your heart. I am in full control. Hold fast for I am with you. Be still, and know that I am God. Am I unable to provide? Your faith is sufficient for Me, so let My faithfulness be sufficient for you.

My purpose and My plan are far beyond your understanding. Although the circumstances of life may tell you otherwise, I shall carry you in peace. Put your hand in Mine, and let Me lead you gently in the way. Put your fears to rest, and find your comfort in My presence. Beloved, I shall save you! Your circumstances matter to Me!

I go through them with you, and I shall not relent until you are delivered. But have the heart to learn from Me in this time. Do not let suffering be without purpose. For I shall use this for good, beginning with giving you a mind of wisdom. Take the time to learn from the circumstance of your life. Gain from My wisdom then apply it.

## *Scripture for Thought*

"Commit your way to the Lord, Trust also in Him, And He shall bring it to pass. He shall bring forth your righteousness as the light, And your justice as the noonday. Rest in the Lord, and wait patiently for Him; Do not fret because of him who prospers in his way, Because of the man who brings wicked schemes to pass. Cease from anger, and forsake wrath; Do not fret—it only causes harm." Psalm 37:5–8

"Mark the blameless man, and observe the upright; For the future of that man is peace. But the transgressors shall be destroyed together; The future of the wicked shall be cut off. But the salvation of the righteous is from the Lord; He is their strength in the time of trouble. And the Lord shall help them and deliver them; He shall deliver them from the wicked, And save them, Because they trust in Him." Psalm 37:37–40

# Day Thirty

# Walk in My Spirit

I do not begin with the outward most places to fill the middle. I consume the internal and shall illuminate the circumference. Let your actions be through My spirit. My Spirit is not glorified when you work through your own devices. I am glorified when you humbly submit. Change your life through changing how you approach Me. Focus on My Spirit, who dwells in you, and allow His light to illuminate your outward parts.

Yes, beloved, let your light so shine before men that they may see My good works through you and glorify the Father who is in heaven. Indeed, My works always glorify My father; therefore let your works be through Me. Surrender yourself, then by a humble walk as you listen to My Holy Spirit, your works shall naturally bring Me joy.

In this, your hand shall become an instrument of My praise. I have chosen you for Myself to bring Me glory. So be a person who is zealous for My good works, not your good works but My good works, which comes through obedience to My Spirit's voice. Be diligent to obey Me, but how can you obey Me unless you're sensitive to My speech?

My child, put your ear to My lips that you can commune with My secrets. Allow Me entrance into the deepest places of your heart that I can consume all the cavities that sin once occupied. How has sin occupied you? Through your disobedience to My voice. But if you always obey My convictions, how shall you stray in the least? Be zealous for Me now. Press forward into the challenge and arise to the occasion. Be diligent to walk in My Spirit without ceasing.

## *Scripture for Thought*

"If we live in the Spirit, let us also walk in the Spirit." Galatians 5:25

Printed in Great Britain
by Amazon